T0197607

My Friend Minnie
(Minnie MeLeah's Invisible Mirror)

To order additional copies of this book, contact:
Xlibris
844-714-8691
www.Xlibris.com
Orders@Xlibris.com

ISBN: Softcover   978-1-4415-9890-5
        EBook   978-1-4771-6625-3

Print information available on the last page

Rev. date: 08/18/2022

My Friend Minnie
(Minnie MeLeah's Invisible Mirror)

Mamie R. Toole

Dedicated
To

Anyone who is intimidated
By other peoples' behaviors

This is a story about a young girl
Minnie MeLeah is her name
She grew up feeling inferior because
Other young folks filled her with shame

She was lonely, and she was frightened
She believed she was inferior
She finally learned what matters most
Is how you view yourself in a mirror

And invisible mirror helped her believe
She was not in a "Nobody" category
She became a "Somebody" everybody wanted to meet
Let her tell you her story

AND REMEMBER—
What matters most is how you see yourself

PREFACE

Look at me
Who I am today
Not an old permanent record account
Of what others had to say

I am here to learn more about
Things I never knew
Don't push me in some corner
I want to learn from you

Please don't be like the others
Who believed what they read
They looked at the last year's record
And they ignored me instead

They allowed other students' behaviors
That kept me so aggravated
And they ignored anything I tried to say
So I felt intimidated

So here I am again
Ready and willing you see
Please put me in my today's mirror
Yesterday's reflection is not today's "Me"

"MY FRIEND MINNIE"

I want to tell you a story
It's really all about me
I was sad or mad most of the time
I was as unhappy as I could be

Inside my head I always thought
No one cared about me
Sometimes I couldn't sleep nor could I eat
My life was such misery

I was walking alone from school one day
When I heard this funny sound
I couldn't concentrate on my lessons and homework
Thinking those mean girls were around

Everybody had wanted to pick on me
Behind the teachers' back
They would push me, and then jump in front of me
To stop me in my tracks

Then they would quietly call me dirty names
So they wouldn't get caught
But when I'd tell whoever was in charge
Everybody would say it was my fault

I wanted them to be my friends
And always took the blame
So they kept on bothering and meddling with me
I kept on feeling ashamed

Then those same funny voices sounded very clear
Hey! Little Girl! What's your name?
I said, "My name is Minnie: Where are you?"
"I am on the ground our name is the same"

"My name is Minnie too"
The voice was very clear
"Look down Minnie—near your feet
Here I am right here"

I looked down and saw this dirty thing
Nearly covered over dirt
"I want to be your friend Minnie" the voice said
"I am tired of seeing you hurt"

I was almost afraid to pick it up
When I saw the dirty face
Gazing up at me from the ground
I was cautious, just in case

"Pick me up! I won't bite you!
I need some warm hands to hold"
So, reluctantly, I picked up that dirty old thing
The voice was right, it was very cold

I thought it was my imagination
And I was going crazy in my head
I closed my eyes and wanted to run
But the voice got louder as it said

"Minnie, I am just a mirror
Wipe me off and I'll be invisible
You'll be the only one who can hear me and see me
But I'll keep you from being so miserable"

"I want to help you see yourself more clearly
Hold me up to your face, I am here"
I said with tears streaming down my face
"Other kids threaten to pull out my hair"

There are so many things they always do
I remember mean things that they say
Then they tell me they're going to beat me up
If I came to school the next day

I felt silly talking to myself
I said, I wish I could keep you forever
The mirror spoke out loud and clear
"Minnie I'll never leave you. Never! Never! Never!"

"I am here to give you confidence
In yourself that you never have had
I'm here to help you believe in yourself
And help you stop looking so sad"

"Look in your mirror and see yourself smile
Laugh at some funny faces you make
People will wonder why they can't make you mad
Just ignore them for goodness sake"

But they make fun of me if I make good grades
They laugh at the clothes I wear
They talk about my parents
They laugh at my long flowing hair

They always talk about me
Always trying to pick a fight
With their hands or mean words they attack me
And I know that it is not alright

"Minnie as your magic mirror your reflection
Should prove just how pretty you can be
It should reflect how life can make changes
Show them that you have dignity"

"I'll be here to tell you Go Minnie!
Go Minnie! Go Minnie! Go!"
"Pull me out of your pocket and look in my face
And you'll learn what you need to know"

"Your so called friends will see your beauty
They will ask you to be their friend
They will wonder why they were mean to you
And how you can look at them now and grin"

"No more will they call you ugly, tall, or skinny
They will ask you to be their friend
They will wonder why they didn't like you
And how you can look at them now and grin"

Their words make me feel like I'm nothing
And feel like I want to cry
Sometimes I just want to run and hide
Or curl up in some corner and die

But I remember that my dad is a preacher
And he tells me examples from God's word
Sometimes I don't think he knows how I feel
Sometimes I pretend I hadn't heard

"Minnie this is the first day of the rest of your life
Don't allow yourself to feel small
You know as much and can do as much as anyone else
Look at the big mirror on the wall"

"You don't have to beg for friendship
You don't have to allow your morals to bend
You don't need to dress fancy or act like them
Floppy and flimsy and showing your skin"

It makes me happy now and when I look at myself
In my imaginary looking glass
I can look like a clown and laugh and laugh
For I know that this look won't last

I look so funny when I make ugly faces
I try to be as ugly as I can be
From now on I'll laugh when other folks lie
And try to paint hateful things about me

I am going to ignore what they try to do
To a young pretty girl my age
I'll tell my friend Minnie I'm not listening
And I'll turn another page

Wow! Look at me! The new real me
I don't want to be like everyone else
I want to be a reflection of a child of God
Minnie, you taught me that yourself

I also kept a prayer in my mind
"Lord, I want to be more like You"
I wiped the dirt off my mirror
And began to see a brand new view

When my mom asks why was I so happy
I said I met a friend just my size
I could hear mom say, "Thank you Jesus"
And sometimes a tear fell from my eyes

I told my mom all about my new friend
I told my sister and brothers too
But when I told my dad
He just said, "Minnie good for you"

I will cherish my new found friend
I'll keep it forever with me
When I brushed off it's dirt, it changed my life
And made my fears and anxieties flee.

I am thankful I have this new found friend
It shows me what I want to see
Freed me from yesterday-prepared me for today and tomorrow
My invisible mirror named "Minnie and Me"

Now when I'm quiet and in my room
And my mirror is in my hand
If my mom yells, "Minnie! What are you doing?"
I say **"Mom, I'm just talking to my Friend."**

Printed in the United States
by Baker & Taylor Publisher Services